Encore

Your favourite ABRSM piano exam pieces

Book 1

CW00448962

6.95

Giga
Third movement from Lesson in C, Op. 12 No. 2

Edited by Richard Jones

Samuel Arnold
(1740–1802)

* Players with small hands may leave out the upper left-hand note.

Samuel Arnold, an English composer who wrote stage works for London theatres, was director of the Academy of Ancient Music and organist at Westminster Abbey.

Even quavers in 6/8 time; melodic sequences; scale and arpeggio patterns.

Recognizing scale and arpeggio patterns and intervals leads to more accurate note-reading. Play a two-octave scale of C major, right and left hands separately, and then look in this piece for scale and arpeggio patterns, and octave intervals.

The Old Cuckoo-Clock

Edited by Richard Jones

Nina M. Bachinskaya
(?–1984)

Nina Bachinskaya was a Russian composer. The music of *The Old Cuckoo-Clock* is a clear depiction of the piece's title, the cuckoo arriving in bar 13.

Even finger staccato; melody in the left hand; accents; keyboard geography (knowing your way around the keyboard).

To develop keyboard geography and staccato touch at speed, play bar 1 on all the Cs and Ds on the piano, staccato, from low to high and high to low, as quickly as you can. Do the same with the notes of bar 6 (staccato E and F♯).

A Song of Erin

No. 8 from *First Year Pieces*

Edited by Richard Jones

Thomas Dunhill
(1877–1946)

Andante con moto [♩ = *c*.120]

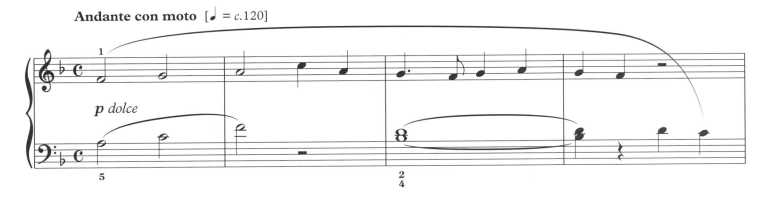

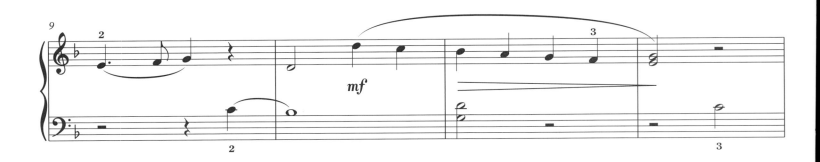

poco rit.

Thomas Dunhill was a British teacher and composer. 'Erin' is another word for Ireland, and the influence of Irish folk melodies can be heard in this piece.

Independence of the hands; creating character through phrasing, dynamics and tempo.

To develop skill in improvisation and composition, compose another melody based on the right hand's notes in bars 1–4 (taken from the pentatonic scale C-D-F-G-A). Give your melody a title.

Cradle Song

No. 17 from *The First Lessons*, Op. 117

Edited by Richard Jones

Cornelius Gurlitt
(1820–1901)

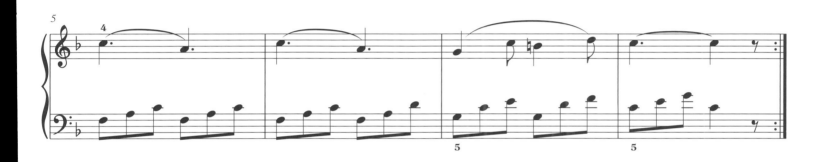

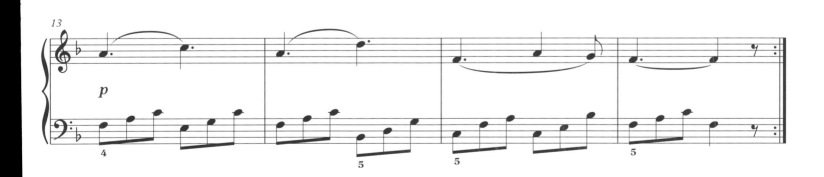

The Danish-born pianist and composer Cornelius Gurlitt taught in Copenhagen and Hamburg. He composed a great number of works.

Rhythms in 6/8 time; balancing melody above an accompaniment; even playing of broken chords; expressing a dynamic range.

Clap the pulse, stressing the first beat of each bar, while your teacher plays the music. Play the left-hand broken chords as solid chords to help develop the correct hand positions. Experiment with the sustaining pedal, and note the difference in sound this creates.

AB 3809

Gavotte

No. 3 from *24 Progressive Lessons*, Op. 81

Edited by Richard Jones

James Hook
(1746–1827)

James Hook was a British composer from Norwich. A gavotte is a French dance in moderate two-time.

Even quaver fingerwork; dynamic range including block dynamics; slurs – couplet (two-note) and longer.

Recognizing musical patterns helps develop accurate playing. Spot the bars that are repeated, and those that are slightly changed. Listen to and play bar 3 then bar 7, for example, and work out where the differences lie.

Theme and First Variation

from *5 Happy Variations on a Russian Folksong*, Op. 51 No. 1

Dmitry Kabalevsky
(1904–87)

Theme

Variation 1

Russian composer Kabalevsky's Op. 51 was inspired by Russian, Slovakian and Ukranian folksongs. Other variations in Op. 51 include Grey Day Variations and Merry Dance Variations.

Keyboard geography with octave leaps; varied articulation (legato; staccato; couplet slurs); fast tempo with many rests.

Research the musical form of theme and variations. Trace the folk melody that is the theme, then see how it is altered in Variation 1. Play the left-hand staccato leaps in high and low octaves on the keyboard, to improve spatial awareness.

AB 3809

The Echo

No. 14 from *Mayflowers*, Op. 61

Edited by Richard Jones

Theodor Oesten
(1813–70)

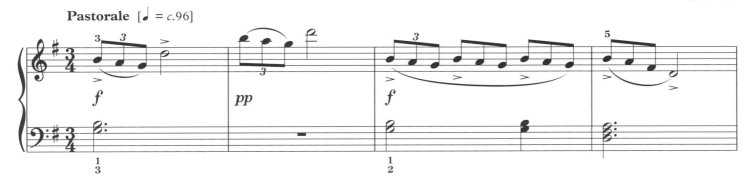

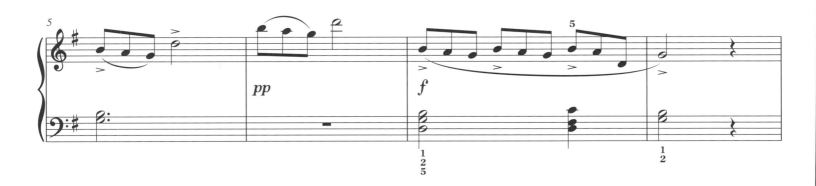

The German pianist, composer and teacher Theodor Oesten studied in Berlin. He wrote many easy piano pieces, and transcriptions from operas.

Sudden contrasting dynamics; counting a triplet in 3/4; fast accurate movement over the keyboard while maintaining pulse.

To develop rhythmic accuracy, clap the music's pulse, one bar *forte* followed by one bar *pianissimo* (the 'echo' of the title). Then try clapping the right hand's rhythm, one bar at a time, each bar repeated as an echo.

African Dance

from *Bigger Picture Piano*, Grade 2–3

John Rowcroft
(born 1970)

Relaxed 'township' feel ♩ = 132

John Rowcroft is a British composer who writes and produces music for film and television. This piece should be rhythmically precise, but have a relaxed South African 'township' feel to it.

Precise chord placement with all notes sounding equally; melody singing through in both bass and treble clefs; accurate long tied notes.

Repeat the piece's first two chords as a left-hand ostinato, and above it make up a tune using the notes A-B♭-C-D-F. Aim for short phrases with a short rest between each one. This will develop improvisation skills.

AB 3809

The Ballet

No. 19 from *60 Pieces for Aspiring Players*, Book 1

Edited by Howard Ferguson

Daniel G. Türk
(1750–1813)

Daniel Türk was a German composer and university professor of music. The delicate quavers are appropriate for a piece entitled 'The Ballet', and perhaps represent skilled footwork.

Freedom in moving around the keyboard; even quaver and semiquaver work; both hands using the treble clef.

To strengthen fingers, and improve articulation using different kinds of touch, make an exercise of bars 9–12 (right hand). The notes are the A major pentachord A-B-C#-D-E. Then, using both hands, play these bars legato/staccato, *piano/forte*, and fast/slow.

AB 3809

Chattanooga Choo Choo

(middle eight)

Arranged by Mark Marshall

Harry Warren (1893-1981) and
Mack Gordon (1904-59)

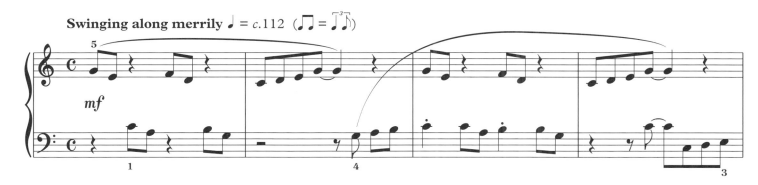

Mark Marshall arranged *Chattanooga Choo Choo* for piano. This well-known American popular song featured in the 1941 film *Sunny Valley Serenade*.

Swung quavers with syncopation; melody passing between hands; varied articulation (staccato, legato and accents).

To understand aurally the difference between swung and straight quavers, play the first phrase both ways and consider how they are different. Listen to a recording of the song *Chattanooga Choo Choo* and think about how the words give character to the music.

Vampire Blues

from *Spooky Piano Time*

Kevin Wooding
(born 1964)

The Australian-born composer Kevin Wooding now lives in the UK. He advises players of this piece to 'count steadily' and 'beware of the vampire's "bite" near the end!'.

Rhythmic and pulse challenges; detailed articulation; keyboard geography; sustaining pedal.

To learn to maintain the pulse when playing difficult rhythms, clap the pulse while your teacher plays the piece. Then listen again, clapping when there is a rest, to help ensure the rests are recognized. Try clapping all the right-hand phrases, and note which rhythms are repeated.

Musette

BWV Anh. II 126
from *The Anna Magdalena Bach Book of 1725*

Edited by Richard Jones

Anon.

D.C. al Fine

A musette is a dance with a drone-like bass line, inspired by the sound of the French 'musette' bagpipes. This piece may have been composed by one of J. S. Bach's sons.

Left-hand octaves with a rotary wrist; playing in similar motion; two-, three- and four-note slurs requiring strong right-hand fingers.

Play the left hand of bars 1 and 2, then using the notes of the D major pentachord (D-E-F#-G-A), compose a different melody over the top. Reinforce the patterns of the piece by exploring the D major scale, using different dynamics and articulation (*forte*; *piano*; staccato; legato).

Adapted from J. S. Bach *et al*, *The Anna Magdalena Bach Book of 1725*, edited by Richard Jones (ABRSM)

AB 3809

Ecossaise in E flat

WoO 86

Edited by Howard Ferguson

Ludwig van Beethoven
(1770–1827)

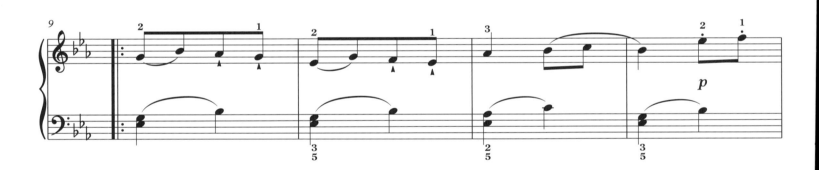

An ecossaise is a dance, usually in a lively two-time. Beethoven also wrote ecossaises for military band and other ensembles.

Varied articulation; use of *sforzando* (*sf*); accurate fingerwork at speed; stylistic, classical phrasing.

To develop awareness of key and the varied articulation and dynamics in the piece, play one octave of the scale of E♭ major staccato then legato, *forte* then *piano*. Also play it using the right hand's articulation in bar 5 – two notes slurred, then two notes detached.

AB 3809

The Prince of Denmark's March

Edited by Richard Jones

Jeremiah Clarke
(c. 1674–1707)

This piece of music by Jeremiah Clarke, formerly known as Trumpet Voluntary, has been famously but wrongly attributed to Purcell. This is a majestic march composed for royalty.

Playing in 2/2; two- (and sometimes three-) part texture (where the hands work independently); ornaments.

Find and listen to recordings of this piece as originally written, to help inspire interpretation of the dynamics, phrasing and articulation of the period. Play the right hand only without the ornaments, then again with the ornaments. Practise both ways with a metronome.

Balletto

Edited by ABRSM

Georg S. Löhlein
(1725–81)

Georg Löhlein was a German composer, teacher and theorist who studied at the universities of Jena and Leipzig. He was well-known for his keyboard method *Clavier-Schule* (1765).

Playing 3rds; varied articulation; different phrase-lengths; interpreting the classical style.

Find the similarities and differences in the music. Identify which bars are repeated, and which are changed in pitch (higher or lower) or rhythm (different rhythmic patterns). Consider how bars 1 and 2 relate to bars 5 and 6, and to bars 9 and 10.

Mozzie

from *Easy Little Peppers*

Elissa Milne
(born 1967)

Elissa Milne is an Australian-based composer and piano teacher who has written more than 100 piano teaching pieces. You can hear the mosquito (mozzie) darting around in this music.

Playing long tied chords; wide range of dynamics and articulation; stylish interpretation of the jazz genre.

It is useful to be able to identify the tools of jazz composition. Note the repeated pattern in bars 1–8 of the left hand (slightly different the second time). Use the notes of the blues scale in D (D-F-G-A♭-A-C) to compose a different left-hand pattern over four bars, and accompany with the right-hand chord D/F.

AB 3809

Cloudy Day

No. 6 from *Microjazz I*

Christopher Norton
(born 1953)

Expressively, with rubato $\textbf{\textit{d}} = c.92$

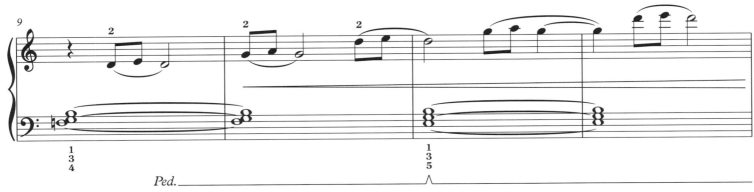

This piece, from Christopher Norton's *Microjazz I*, is in a contemporary style, and provides evocative musical pictures of a cloudy day.

Playing varied articulation above chordal pedal notes; pedal used as an effect; rubato; large leaps around the keyboard.

While your teacher plays the music, clap the pulse of two-in-a-bar. Note when you hear differences in articulation (staccato and legato), and when the pedal is used. To develop expressive playing, try imagining, or drawing, a picture that will go with the music.

Fingering is editorial.

AB 3809

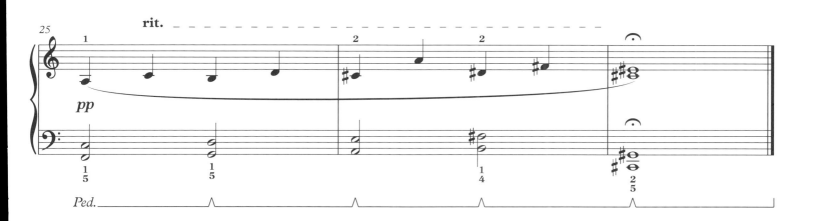

The Bee

from *Fantasy Studies for the Second Year*, Op. 13

Edited by Richard Jones

Alec Rowley
(1892–1958)

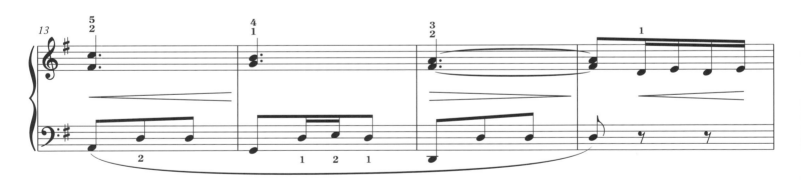

Alec Rowley was an English composer, pianist and teacher who was professor at Trinity College of Music from 1919. He mainly wrote educational music.

Even semiquaver work in both hands; melody crossing between the hands; playing accurate rhythms with frequent changes in note values.

Find and listen to a recording of the orchestral interlude 'Flight of the Bumble Bee' by Rimsky-Korsakov. Consider how this is different to Rowley's piano piece, and how a composer uses different techniques to illustrate a title in sound.

Fingering is editorial.

AB 3809

Lullaby

No. 5 from *Six Sketches*

Edited by Richard Jones

Charles V. Stanford
(1852–1924)

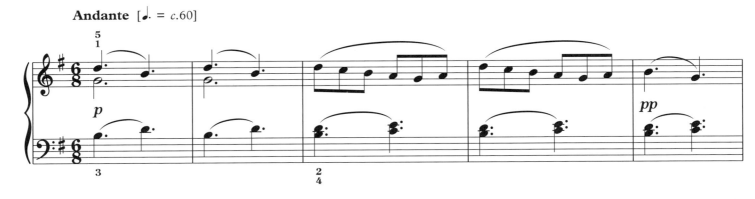

Charles Stanford was an Irish composer and teacher who was a professor at both Cambridge University and the Royal College of Music. This lullaby imitates a rocking cradle.

Part-playing; slurs; extensive quiet dynamics; legato chords placed accurately with notes together.

Link the feel of two-in-a-bar (in 6/8 time) to the motion of a cradle by rocking your arms, or moving from one foot to another as you listen to your teacher play the music. To develop listening skills, work out the similarities and differences between this lullaby and Gurlitt's *Cradle Song* (see page 5).

AB 3809

Strange Things Happen

Sarah Watts

The jazz and educational composer Sarah Watts studied bassoon and piano at the Royal College of Music. Her publications include the *Red Hot Recorder* and *Razzamajazz* series.

Varied articulation; syncopation, with swung quavers and precise chords.

Play the walking bass line of bars 9–12. Compose a right-hand part to go over this, using chords from the piece and part of the D blues scale (D-F-G-A♭). This will help develop improvisation and composition skills, as well as build understanding of the walking bass, a jazz technique.

AB 3809

Garage Sale

from *Really Easy Jazzin' About*

Pam Wedgwood
(born 1947)

🔖 Pam Wedgwood is a UK-based teacher and composer who has composed a large amount of popular educational music. She suggests this piece needs a 'heavy rock' rhythm.

🎹 Precise, well-coordinated finger work; varied articulation; syncopation and accented two-note chords.

💡 To develop skill at playing by ear, play the left-hand notes of bars 1–3 in the right hand, without looking at the music. Record your playing, and check if you played the correct rhythm and articulation when you listen to the recording.

AB 3809